Also by Dan Bellm

A Story in a Bottle (chapbook, 1991)
Terrain (chapbook, with Molly Fisk and Forrest Hamer, 1998)
Buried Treasure (forthcoming, 1999)

TRANSLATION:
Angel's Kite / La Estrella de Angel, by Alberto Blanco (1994)

Dan Bellm

One Hand on the Wheel

THE ROUNDHOUSE PRESS

Publisher's Cataloging-in-Publication Data
Bellm, Dan.
One hand on the wheel / Dan Bellm — 1st ed.
p. cm. — (California poetry series ; #1)
ISBN: 0-9666691-0-X
1. Fathers and sons — Poetry.   2. San Francisco (Calif.) — Poetry.
3. Gays' writings, American.   I. Title.
PS3552.E53375O54 1999   811'.54
QBI99-252

Several of the poems in this book, often in earlier versions, first appeared in the following magazines: *Estero:* "Fighting with the dead"; *Ploughshares:* "Brightness"; *Poetry:* "Before words," "Homage"; *Poetry Now:* "Nashvillanelle"; *River Styx:* "Boy wearing a dress"; *The Santa Clara Review:* "Damage"; *The Taos Review:* "I think we're alone now" (as "May '68"); *TriQuarterly:* "Illinois River."

The epigraphs to the six sections of the book appeared as part of "9 poems" in the chapbook, *Terrain* (Nevada City, CA: Hip Pocket Press, 1998), along with "Before words," "Boy wearing a dress," "Brightness," "Illinois River," "Lament" and "Nashvillanelle."

"Damage," "I think we're alone now" (as "May '68") and "Midrash of the abandoned child" appeared in earlier form in the chapbook, *A Story in a Bottle* (San Francisco: Norton Coker Press, 1991). "Boy wearing a dress" was reprinted in the *San Francisco Bay Guardian.* "Book of maps (3)" and "Boy wearing a dress" also appeared in *A Day for A Lay: A Century of Gay Poetry* (New York: Barricade, 1999).

The poems "Homage," "Before words," "Damage" and "Lament" have been set to music by the composer Jorge Martín, the latter three in a sequence entitled "Of Fathers and Sons."

Note: A *midrash* is a Jewish legend or commentary written in response to a Biblical text, often arising from an urge to tell an untold part of a familiar story.

My deepest thanks for helping to bring this book to life: Molly Fisk, Forrest Hamer, the Squaw Valley Community of Writers, Joyce Jenkins, Malcolm Margolin, and most of all, Yoel Kahn.

This is Volume 1 of the California Poetry Series.
Series editor: Joyce Jenkins
Cover Photo: Christopher Felver
Author Photo: Sam Fisk
Cover and Interior Design: David Bullen Design

Orders, inquiries, and correspondence should be addressed to:
California Poetry Series
c/o The Roundhouse Press
P.O. Box 9145
Berkeley, California 94709
phone: 510.549.3564 fax: 510.549.1889
e-mail: roundhouse@heydaybooks.com

Printed in Canada
10   9   8   7   6   5   4   3   2   1

For Yoel and Adam   and in memory of my father, C.V. Bellm
December 7, 1922–August 3, 1994

Sólo el amor con su ciencia
nos vuelve tan inocentes
VIOLETA PARRA

Contents

nothing but horizon, Dad, laid bare by pioneers like you—

Hands

Here, scarred over nicely, is where the tip was sawed away — Working
yourself down to bone there were bound to be accidents
in the tender places — Here, the thumb of your right hand
got reattached, but at a slant: I like to imagine I feel
a lost tenderness coming to you again
as the tension drains from your fingers — I mean, the life — the two of us holding

hands like little brothers, and though you don't hold
mine back you can't pull yours away. Whole days I sit and do the work
of talking for the both of us, easier now, knowing you won't wake again,
but I think you hear me, thanking, forgiving — no accident
it's me, Dad, your mortal enemy and friend — I think you can feel
my hands in yours, bone to bone, your hands

going cold on me that were so strong your handshakes
hurt but I could kill you now, I could hold
you down and make you stay, make you feel
proud of me that for once I'd done some real work
with my hands — Oh wait — I only notice by accident
you were gone a minute — you've started breathing again,

that relinquishing groan, your last lung rising up against
the bedsheet, your mouth the gaping O of a saint handing
over his life in a trance, Isaac blessing the second son by accident,
fooled by blindness — Did I scare you? — Don't go — I haven't held
your hands since I was a child, they're so cool and soft, but that's death, working
harder even than you — It's strange — I didn't know I'd feel

happy in the end and does it mean our struggle is done that I feel
happy, with your blessing or not, not really wanting you back again
but wanting the farewell to last? I see you leaving for work,
the unresponding God eternally going away, your hands
in fists. I see you one afternoon in '68 holding
two fists in the air and crying in shame — there's been an accident —

the radiator cap as you turned it flew up by accident
and boiling fluid sprayed over your hands — as much as the pain you feel
ashamed to be crying, and mad that I saw, and turn your back. I see you holding
one hand down to hammer and hack and burn it again
and again, see you lifting more weight into your hands
than your back can hold. O discoloring skin, unmarrowing bone, o working

armor: any baby, first thing, will grasp at a touch and hold on but I feel
your hands now working themselves away, unfathering me — What an accident
of death that they begin to look like infant hands, as if you will live again.

Though we are not through with him he is through with us —

he walks out of the picture at left, head down
into bright sun, holding the ache in his side,

seizes the moment when we're facing
another direction to slip
away, as the old and weary sometimes do,
shivering to be warm, heading
south —

I suppose he will want to drive there,
yes — finds the dead car
his dead father left him
out back behind the age-old mound
of undiscardable scrap,

climbs into that plush-lined boat
with the automatic windows and doors
and it starts —

it's just where he wants to be,
nothing to do but watch
and his attention becomes the road ahead,
his thoughts
are light —

he crosses the river at Paducah
without waving back,

he doesn't remember us. He remembers
the salt ocean
and the way there is clear

though he becomes smaller the farther he goes

so the longer he is gone the distance is greater

and it will take him forever
and he has forever,

stopping now and then at roadside places
for the pleasure of talking
with the other dead.

Lament

There should be more empty space on the paper

There should be more empty space / than there was / before I wrote on it

I should clear the words away / to make space for the words unsaid / the words set aside / the words forgotten

I should leave the paper whiter than it was

I should make more room between the lines / for the intervals between words that last years / the indentations / the foreshortenings / the cropped borders

It should be plain what could have been written but was not / for loss of time / for theft of life

There should be fewer words now / for the sake of the one who has died / without a word / the way a gate shuts / the way time disappears / into heaven

There should be more silence for him / the one taught to ask less / told to wait without hope / left to comfort himself / who decided to tell no one / decided again every day / to tell no one

There should be more empty space on the paper / for the blessing choked back / for good

There should be a blinding darkness

A terrible / soundless / whirlwind / erasing

Hardly any use to look for her inside it; hard to say,
turning the all-alike pages, what she'd remember
if she read it now, which anyway she won't — she didn't write
in it to ever read it back exactly, and now she keeps it down
on a low shelf in the front room where any time she wants she
can see it plain without having to look inside, a spiral stenographer's notebook

we poked fun at growing up — (sold as "A Superior Notebook
With Leaves That Turn Fast and Lie Down Flat") — it said
so little — just names of places she
and Dad had eaten and slept at and how much they cost and numbers to remember
the kind of time they'd made and the mileage on the car, the cover creased down
at one corner but still sturdy after 17 years of writing

in motel rooms at night or a moving car, *1948 to 1965* written
at the top and the whole thing held shut with a rubber band, the notebook
my mother started on her wedding night: *Tuesday March 30 Sundown*
Auto Court west of St. Louis $4.00, she wrote, and chose to say
nothing more, which made me figure there was nothing to remember.
One day they took photos of each other: him squinting like a boy into the sun, she

in a jaunty head scarf at a guardrail in a good wind — you can see she
feels radiant but holds a little radiance back. That night she wrote,
Dan-Dee Court $3.50 mileage 25916 lunch at the Embers
in Flagstaff while we had the car greased — the notebook
skipping right over the Grand Canyon like a '46 Kaiser making good time and
                                                              declining to say
what it thought or felt as they flew all the way to California down

Route 66, stopping now and then in Little Rock or Yuma to hunt down
an Army pal — an outlandish adventure for people of their class. She
was a stenographer at a truck depot when they met and, driving through, he'd
                                                              stop to say
hello and catch her off guard a little as she worked; she wrote

good shorthand and typed fast and must have thought, notebook
poised mid-air, she could handle him fine though he looked a little rough, remembering

her drunken stepdad. Not long ago I asked her, So as a kid do you remember
confiding in anybody if you couldn't go to your Mom, and she looked so downcast
I wanted to unask it — *No* — *not really* — *I guess* — *no* — The book
she'd been reading froze in her hand. Tears glistened. Her husband was dead. I know
she'd

say she was happy enough those years — she answers only *I get along all right*
if I try to be a comfort. More than that she finds it better not to say,

smoothing the tablecloth with a cupped hand long after it lies down
flat. She taught me herself to grow up quietly, carefully, not to say
too much. She taught me to write down what I remember in a book.

Funeral flowers: two sisters still not speaking

Discipline

What he had to teach I didn't want to learn,
what I wanted to learn he was not the one to teach,
and we turned from each other with a graceless dismay,
heartsore, hurt-shy, trapped together in a family; I thought,
I am not the kind of boy he wished
for, if he made a wish; I thought it was my job to give

him happiness. I studied his face, and saw that his eyes gave
off darkness, and saw that he knew I saw, and learned
to stand back from it and look away, wishing
light to appear, some sign, some relenting of dread. He taught
me to fetch things without names — head under the truck hood — *Thought
I told you the other one goddamn it* — lip flared in disgust —

Now put that away and bring me what I want. I learned to disappear
from his regard, into the house, into a book, someplace he would give
no thought to me, unnecessary child, anonymous boy, thinking,
I will read the World Book Encyclopedia beginning to end and learn
what there is to know with no one's help; I will teach
myself where to go and how to live. He taught me that wishing

is grief. He taught me orderliness and anguish,
hard work and hopelessness in equal parts, discipline
and doubt, the sure belief it was impossible to teach
me anything, better just to do it himself. He gave
me his loneliness, but withheld how to use it, and I learned
to take refuge with women, and his rage sparked more: he thought

I would abandon him and I did, a child with thoughts
in his head and the hands of a girl. He didn't wish
his own life on me, but what was there to learn
out of books worth his paying for in sweat? Disrespect
and laziness, big-ass complicated five-dollar words — *Give
you everything you want too fast is the trouble. Ought to teach*

you to work, way my father did. Ashamed underneath how teachers
had left him in back for lost, never thought
to ask themselves if he could read, or noticed his hands had a gift
for taking things apart and putting them right. I only wished
he would say he loved me, but I don't think he did; no dishonor
in admitting it now; same went for his father too. We learned

to give up on each other, learned to avoid the thoughts
and wishes in each other's eyes, but not to give in, not to forgive.
We were taught very strictly to stay dissatisfied.

She wants him to write a letter home to his father, she wants him
      to make peace — *Please tell him at the least about this place*
we've come to — A crossroads of mud, a flatland so fearfully
      unrelieved, so unbounded, too far from trade and life
to have promise as a town. No land of their own. *High Land:*
      he can hear his father and brother pronounce the name
with scorn, a name coined by deceivers to make the Swiss think of
      Switzerland, a depression in the earth, a crossroads
placed wrong like a father's second son, like a man with no
      money left him to return home, who will have to make his way.
I was unwanted there, I was placeless in that world,
      a brute animal laboring in his yard. A small man with
enormous hands. He knows he is not clever. He works clearing land
      on a German farm to the north of town where the prairie ends
in forest — an ox dragging stumps. In the summer he joins the hired army
      building the National Trail so the ones who are braver
can travel west. She is learning to make tallow candles like an American,
      and homespun shirts; she gathers wild fruit from the prairie
called *Looking-Glass,* and yellow daisies, and purple mint; he knows
      he cannot complain of her, though disappointment has made them
silent. So fearless when they met in school, so ready to come away
      with him — he knows his anger wearies her. *I think you were born*
dissatisfied — write a letter to your father — tell him at the least
      of your hopes — ask for his prayers. When he prays with her at dusk
he feels his faith fall from him, leaving the absence which will be God
      henceforth, hopes without joy — a lowland overgrown with grass,
good land but fearfully lonesome, so fraught with impediments
      to clear away. Some men on the road sing German songs
and the Americans like to work alongside, it is so cheerful, but he stays
      apart, though he knows the words. One day he took out his
German watch for them, the silver chain slender as the lifeline of his hand;
      an American wanted it for his wedding-day but when it returned
he could see it had been taken apart, as if the fool had wished
      to examine its soul. He will waste no more time with fools.
His grandfather's watch, his only inheritance — now they are twice dead,
      the generations of whom no record was kept. Alone, going out

into the dawn with his gun, he can think of childhood mischief with a smile,
    the trouble he got away with rare times, the day the other boys
dared him to jump from the barn roof into snow. *Summon your courage*
    she tells him, *write to your father and brother, tell them at the least*
we're going to have a child. He supposes no one will recall him either;
    his children will be Americans; one day his timepiece
will be a stilled face, exhausted from within; the town will not prosper,
    because it is located wrong. *But I will not write. No,*
they will not hear a word. I will not tell them pleasant lies about America.
    Let them wonder what became of me.

He appears at the kitchen door out back like a stranger,
　　　　like a hobo with his hand out but staggers into the house
to catch his balance, the other hand at his side to hold the pain
　　　　in, his face battered so red the children stand back,
the youngest not even sure who it is, it has been so long. *Why good Lord.*
　　　　Now what have you done to yourself. Sleepless as a ghost. Sacrificing his life
for a living. Quick she draws a glass of water from the jug, his postcard
　　　　still on the oilcloth of the table pencilled in that labored
childlike hand, addressed to himself his own name spelled wrong —
　　　　Akron O. Got here about 4:30 Will live Monday. From Athur.
My father a nine-year-old boy runs out to the truck to look
　　　　and comes back out of breath, afraid for him, and envious —
he will never live up to a man like this — his father's hands so cold
　　　　they shake. *Three o'clock in the morning I wake up*
rolling over the left shoulder straight for a tree and when
　　　　I whipped it to the right it turned me over
down a seven-foot bank wheels up cab and all — I was caught
　　　　in there. The gas run over me. There were sparks.
I got to the battery and broke the cable off, well what could I do
　　　　I sat on the bank waiting till the morning. Scrape
up his leg and a crack in the ribs. Well what can you do with him.
　　　　She makes a plate of food and watches him eat, puts him to bed
while the oldest runs into town for the doctor four miles. He lives
　　　　a charmed life. His children standing at the door looking in
love him. Half-abandoned months on end on the failing farm, she loves him,
　　　　so recklessly tough he is almost crazy, so disregarding of his body
and his fate. He will live a long life, survive if nothing else
　　　　as a character in his own story, as all his stories are about himself
and his truck, not his wife and children, not his thoughts
　　　　or his heart. There it sits in the yard his truest love with its
windshield out, a three-ton '29 Dodge with hydraulic brakes. A wonder
　　　　they got it winched back upright more or less in one piece
and what does he do, gets back behind the wheel
　　　　and drives it all day and night where another man might
toss in a match and let the insurance worry but no,
　　　　overloaded to high heaven with rubber tires to make the most

for his time, the end gate and the tarpaulin strained to breaking —
        they'll dock his pay he isn't there tomorrow. Now you know
he won't listen to any doctor — minute he's halfway patched
        he'll go on his way, no secret he prefers to be alone, gone,
driving somewhere fast — at nightfall he'll put on a clean set of clothes,
        light up the coal in the side-lanterns, back it into the road
and roar, 600 more miles to Oklahoma City, staring at the dark,
        thinking whatever it is he thinks about.

I think the end of our road must be near at hand,
Dad, and here is a sign, a wall of new snow here to Jerome stopping
our path though below us spring has come to the desert
again, the cholla that poisons its surroundings, like you, so nothing can
come near, blossoming, as ever, though older
than us all, because it was meant to, even if nothing living lasts —

You snarl, at no one, *Now we've accomplished nothing,* and I think, *It's the last
time I get into a car with you I swear* — hand over hand
at the wheel you skid out a U-turn, flinging rock, and then your old
silence falls over us, again, in the recirculated air — If only we could stop
hating before we die, but the baby cries himself awake and I can't
comfort him and you shout *Hush,* though all he has done to deserve

your venom so young is to have a father like me, and Mom, deserted
beside you, implores herself to think of something good. At last
a roadside cafe rises out of the fog like the gate of heaven, or hell — who can
know without entering first? — emblazoned with a waving neon hand,
so you declare *It's time for lunch,* and you pull over, and we stop.
It's 10:30 in the morning. At the counter a line of old

truckers like you are stirring and stirring black water, retelling old
news and wrecks of fate and freaks of weather in the desert
and road conditions and all this rain — You would like to stop
and talk with them, your truer family, I know, but we take the last
table in back and sit, speechless with dread. The baby tears his napkin and hands
you a piece of it, to play, but you fold your arms and glare — you can't

stand it — so long ago you said *I'll tell you what's wrong with the way you live, you can't
give me grandchildren like your brother did* but here is a child, an old
soul staring into your eyes, and Mom reaches over a hand
to accept the gift instead. Down there in the desert
tonight we will have the worst and last
battle of our lives; I will wedge my body in your door to stop

you from closing it on me and when I ask *Can we stop*
fighting now? — you know that life is short — you will shout *I do* not *have cancer,*
that's only what all of you think. "Only the spaces within will last,
where human lives are lived, not walls, not stones," old
Frank Lloyd said, who made his shelter in the unforgiving desert
we drive down into under a heavy sky, the thorn-covered hands

of desert roses opening red in the rain, and I fear the end is at hand,
grandfather, unappeasable old man at the wheel who can't
stop driving and driving and rest in the only heaven we have at last.

solace, worst enemy, mirror ghost father

Consolation

Et exspecto resurrectionem mortuorum,
et vitam venturi saeculi.

After I kiss his forehead lightly once
goodbye,

after the closing of the box,

where does his suffering go —
of course it's the Catholic heaven
he expects, the resurrection of the body
and the life of the world to come

but where does his suffering go —

I mean whatever of it
that is not part of me —

The fearsomeness of his face has been
drained now and recomposed,
injected with a semblance of spirit,
the lips held shut, so like himself,
but with a semblance of rest

because in heaven
the pain of the body and soul is supposed
to be forgotten and past but is it lost,

or does it suffer without him on earth
and where does it remain
to wait
for more life —

Most of the universe is missing
but it isn't lost,
I expect it's here somewhere, world without end,
hiding in plain sight,

all the suffering banished from God's heaven,
all the imploded substance
and the trapped light.

What a poor heaven this earth is —
I would gladly invent another —
but what good is that
to send you to a reward
in my mind —

Will there be one then
and what can I give you
to make up for
— what —
the barrenness of your life
that perhaps is my invention too —

A few days after you were gone
we found a handful of stones
in a drawer —
Mom knew at once
where they came from

but how can we know what they are —

ordinary and neutral-toned and small
each marked in your hand
with the year you
picked it up along a path
at your church retreat house
in spring

and looked at it and held it
and held it in your pocket
an unhurtable thing
that marked the passing

of what was past
and promised
as you prayed

— but I am still inventing —
a way to heaven
stone by stone

Three days after your death the house you
raised us in goes up for sale, and a sign goes up
on the lawn I tended and greened those misspent
Sundays and Saturdays of youth for you, a field gone
brown in giant patches now like dust. Twenty years away and here
I am as if I own the place, as it to claim a body once the life

has fled. Of course I walk right in; of course our life
in it has gone all disremembered since — a red-brick split-level you
built on a re-seeded quarter-acre lot here
at the formerly new edge of town, kids biking home up
the shabby street and it's wretched to feel as gone
as you, to see how others have papered us over with new mistakes,

the telephone you poured your rage into missing
from the kitchen wall, a realtor seated in your living-
room spot with a fact sheet and an asking price, saying *This one'll go
in a hurry* to a frowning man who doubts it, hand on the door, and your
classy oak veneer panelling in the den blotched up
with a soulless wash of white, but look in the basement here,

they've saved your very goofiest home improvement, where
I'd have thought anyone would rip it out without a moment's misgiving:
orange naugahyde built-in sofas with end tables of gold-flecked formica, up-
to-date more or less in 1964, the hideaway where I saved my life
from you. Who will love it now? Here is the door where you
walked out on me, and the window where I watched you go;

what a relief that, after all, that time and place are gone
and I don't want them back, don't care to stay here
any longer, though I have never stopped talking to you
nor you to me, two misfits
on earth unable to share a roof but forever living
in the halves of the same soul. Whenever you fall silent I hold up

your end; I know you're thinking, *People don't keep their property up
any more,* but nothing is ours, Dad, not the shutters and doors gone
unpainted a shade too long, not the battered shrubbery or the grass. That life
is over now. We will never see it again. Your name there
on a stone, the narrow plot you've fallen into by mischance —
I know it isn't much, but for awhile yet you will live in me, I will be your

home. I remember the mystery it was, a house rising up
all new from the open pit I used to play inside, and you standing here
in the doorway, measuring and re-measuring the life to come.

I'm writing what you asked for after all.
She said, "There's a kind of beautiful damage" — I had to say,
I wouldn't call the *damage* beautiful —

"In your poem." Hard words mourning the hard fall
From childhood. A powerful Dad who forced his way.
I'm writing what you asked for. After all

This time — throwing me out for good — I hear him yell
Down the stairs at my brother, "Don't *you* turn out gay."
I wouldn't call the damage beautiful,

And even if beauty *is* truth, truth beauty, I won't call
The damage a gift. Recovery, revenge, is that why
I'm writing? What you asked for, after all —

"Save what you just told her. Use it" — well,
What's the use? I want him back. If I could make him pay,
I wouldn't. Call the damage beautiful,

Admire the fury in a banished soul
Brought up right. When I hear orders, I obey.
I'm writing what you asked for after all.
I wouldn't call the damage beautiful.

it's here somewhere it's only lost

Winter past, floodwaters drawn back, new heat rising
      from Mississippi mud, we sit like brooding gods
on a high rock in the bluffs all Saturday afternoon
      above the river and school and the playing fields,
above the muddy rugs and chairs and boxes of clothes
      baking in the sun on the front lawns of people
washed out every year, too poor to move. How
      generous he is to be my friend, a year ahead of me,
a senior, handsome as a pretty girl. He could be
      anyone's friend. We have my radio tuned
to the Chicago station, the great world flooding small-town
      silence. What you want, baby I got it. Buzzing
flies in the haze of sun on damp grass. Books for
      Sarge's religion class. Black Rage. Why We Can't
Wait. Sodas and Lucky Strikes. Jerry reading me
      a letter from his girlfriend about
decorating the gym for the prom but I'm
      facing Colonel DeVito in his office again
to tell him I'm quitting ROTC, waving a note from home
      with nervous hands, watching his smirk when I say
as a Catholic I'm opposed to war. Being Catholic
      wasn't really my reason but I got the idea from
Sarge when he went on that prayer fast. A Marine
      before he was a priest. He said he was having
a crisis of heart. What was pissing the colonel off
      was I was the guy who took his daughter
to the Military Ball, some kind of Communist.
      What it is ain't exactly clear. There's a
man with a gun over there. Got any idea
      how many Catholic wars there've been, son?
The crew-cut no-neck in the training movie
      looked no older than us, leading the bayonet
charge and jabbing sandbag dummies with a grin.
      Injustice at the heart of things, like a sorrow
in your body. Across the meadow a cow's skull
      stares from a barbed wire fence. I wrote

on the open book exam, I refuse to participate,
		suddenly fearless. I know Jerry's real
best friend is Art who is more of a guy and I'm
		the odd man out, learning to tone myself down
and drop my voice and fit, but I'm popular on
		the dance floor with girls, and suddenly alive.
The sun makes me think of touching myself
		alone in my room. Love is passing me by,
a revolution of love in Madison and Paris, France.
		David told me he never masturbated in his life,
I say, do you believe him? At my last confession,
		the priest breathing close at the dark screen
with questions. Is there anything more you want to
		talk to me about? Are you going through
changes in your body? Are you troubled by impure
		thoughts? I like this freedom, sitting above
the world as if the horizon is my future, the wide
		river's path around a ridge of blue hills where
I can't see. I was walking there by the tracks
		when the radio said King was dead. People set
whole cities on fire but it was quiet here still like
		peace had come, like no one noticed. Poor Sarge,
breaking down in class about passing his prime at a
		boarding school, teaching the privileged to pray
while the sons of the poor go to war. I ask Jerry
		What are you going to do if they draft you?
His cousin in Khe Sanh says you can always get
		a desk job if you're smart. The guy from
the Draft Resistance said you can get an undesirable
		if you tell them you're homo but
it's right there on your draft card forever and besides
		I'm not like that. Was he? We fixed up
the basement of the dorm for him like a coffee
		house. We sang I'm only eighteen, I got a
ruptured spleen and I always carry a purse.
		Strange quivering inside, like the plucking

of strings. What'll you do now my blue-eyed son.
What'll you do now my darling young one.
That was the night David and George, the two biggest
queers in school, swiped the flag and
painted it black in their room, ran it back
up the pole where the whole school saw it on
Sunday morning, like a revolution. It's four o'clock.
It's time for the top ten. I am aware of Jerry's
body near me in the heat, aware of shame. A couple
of women are sweeping muddy gravel out of a
basement down there. What a wreck. What a bad
fate. Next month Jerry will graduate, shake
my hand and leave me behind. No, he doesn't
love me that way because he can't, because it's
impossible. I think we're alone now, there doesn't
seem to be anyone around. I think we're alone now,
the beating of my heart is the only sound.

1.

If I close my eyes now, wherever
I point my finger — the child
has hauled the heavy book of maps
down from its shelf, alone in the house
on a summer day, quiet and alone, the way
he likes to be — *whatever word*

I land on will be home. He feels any word
will do — the pages make a fan — for anywhere
on earth makes a hope of another way
out for a child
not at home in his father's house.
Here is the world etched into shapes on maps:

green and violet: yellow and red: the maps
are places in his mind: picture-words:
each shape a house
no one will harm him in. *This is where*
I'll live when I grow up — the child
has found under the swollen lip of Norway

a name he can't pronounce — *or here,* away
at a tear on the opposite end of the map,
Tierra del Fuego, whose fire is ice. The child
closes his eyes to see the words
lit in reverse inside his head; he doesn't know where
else to look. He likes to dream the house

has a secret room; he likes to dream the house
grows infinitely smaller and blows away,
an island in the blue paper sea where
no one lives, a speck on the map
a hand could erase. Not a word
of what he thinks to anyone. This is how the child

lives. This is how the child
hides in the house
while his father hammers out back hurling words
of damnation at the heat. Keeping out of the way.
He opens his eyes to the place on the map
where he lives as the door slams. *Now where*

is that child? You better tell me where
you're at, cooped up in the house like a goddamn girl. At a word
he rises to be punished, hiding the book of maps away.

2.

If I listen harder — if I become nothing — I'll hear
the voice of God. If I hear the voice of God
I'll be forgiven, so I can live. The child
has learned there is a stain in the soul,
the unfindable soul — is it inside his body? But there's no
answer. If he had the power

of the little-boy saint in the book, the power
to be nothing but a vessel of God, what would he hear?
— the saint who walked to school in prayer showing no
fear of the little classmates about to stone him, only God
in his heart and the fear of God, so that his soul
arose straight to the arms of Jesus, who became a little child

for us. In the cold-brick church the child
held in place between his father's power
and his mother's silence hears nothing. Perhaps his soul
is lost, and God does not want him to hear.
Is he supposed to feel the breath of God
over his face and how will he know

it is God's breath, how will he know
it from the devil's? If a father doesn't love his child
should the child pray to the sorrowful Mother? But if God
is disappointed what power
does a crying mother have to make him hear?
The boy has nightmares in which his soul

freezes like breath: the painted Jesus sees into his soul
from the wall in the dark, and moves to harm him, no
light in his eyes. He wakes before he can hear
the curse in words, but he hears it: *Foolish child,
I have done everything in my power
for your love. I am an angry God.*

The boy is folding his hands to appear devout in God's
house, but he is tired of trying to pray, his soul
is already stopping believing in its power
to speak. The soul has a stain, and if no
one will love it he will live without love, like a child
who has become nothing. *If I am still enough will I hear*

*what God wants? Will my soul
rise to heaven on the power of grace?* The child
folds his hands. If he hears no answer, is the answer *No?*

3.

*If I'm not a strong person — if I'm not like other
boys — maybe I shouldn't have been a boy
at all.* In his halflit room the child
is looking at his body
with his brand-new glasses off. Here
he can be as invisible as he wants. Yes,

it's getting harder to see; yes,
his vision will be bad forever; yes, the others

will outrace him as he feels his way. Here,
held up a little closer than before, are a girl's
hands, not the hands of his father — anybody
can see how the bones could break. Sensitive child —

oversensitive — you can't let the other children
make you cry his mother says — *Ignore them, yes,*
that's what I did in school. He wishes his body
could be solider or disappear when the other
boys come at him at the schoolyard door, one boy
most of all who spits, says *faggot* and *girl,* who hit him here

in the chest until he did cry, and here
on his girl-limp arms. His body is not his hope. The child
supposes if he were a girl
the other boys might like him then, yes,
might even apologize, and he would like the other
boys to care for him, one most of all whose body

is mean and shines with sweat, him more than anybody,
and the child touches himself here
where his legs join while the other
hand strokes the rising — um — the child
doesn't yet call it anything to himself — yes —
until he shivers to a stop, imagining the boy

beside him, *but I would have to be a girl*
for that, and I'm not, I have this puny body
of a boy. Then hope must lie in his mind, yes,
all right, he can see more clearly in here
with his bad eyes shut, child
who would rather have any other

body but his own, girlboy
given to see the world as through a glass, but here
is his body and he will live in it, yes, because there is no other.

Midrash of the abandoned child | *San Francisco, 1991*

He is standing on a busy streetcorner
where a massive brick building meets the sidewalk

making gestures of war
to no one or to no one visible

kicking and wheeling
wildness in his eyes and hair

as if he is set upon on all sides
because he is

because he is abandoned to a danger of his own
like you

child, whose parents are unknown
like the parents of the first of your name

a story buried away
before the story began —

could be they were a little
crazy, unpresentable, unfit —

and you were set down in their stead to prosper
adopted by God as if born to God

in Paradise, a garden
lost, it's said, because of you

for your wanting to know something
so complicated

as where you came from
and who made you

only the place name passed down in writing
for memory

here in second earth
where birth is made sweat

and life one long day of work a parent leaves
as a child enters, with a screaming

cry, and I see the man is screaming
though he makes no sound

and I imagine it's because
he has lost his child

is too forlorn
to care for his child

has walked away from the hospital police desk
into complete night

and is bereft of you
my love

who have come instead to me
marked with history

but set down adrift without it.

Boy wearing a dress

On the way home he asks me, *If we cut off our*
penises then we'd be girls wouldn't we Dad,
my little boy in cowboy boots and a long black dress
walking home from Castro Street playing
blue fairy and wicked stepsister and lost princess as he
walks, the people and store windows whirling by

as he twirls only figures in fairy stories he knows by
heart, though what he doesn't see yet is that our
neighborhood's a kind of fairyland for real — still, I hope no one heard him
ask me that, and hope my Dad
who is dead hasn't heard, who would never have let me play
boy and girl with this frightening freedom, dressing

up in public or alone in a four-dollar thrift-store dress
we bought because he asked for one. A drunk careening by
asks, *Why who are you some kind of superhero, son,* and from a display
window video porno stars sweating under harsh light smirk in our
faces — *I don't have to tell them who I am now do I Dad* —
No it's a dress, the guy's friend says, *I've seen him*

around before, that boy's always in costume, he
must be a little fag. Ken dolls in white satin dresses
and angel wings and hairless Barbies done up as leather Dads
are climbing a Christmas tree inside the card shop by
the pizza store, some queen's fantasy scenario of what our
mothers and fathers should have let us play

back where we come from, but my little boy likes to play
the girl parts of stories for reasons of his own, he
likes their speeches and their dresses and shoes, we tell ourselves
it's harmless, wanting to wear a dress,
harmless as my nervous laughter to passersby
and what do I apologize to them for, Dad —

When I was a child I wanted to wear my Dad's
work shirts, I liked the smell of his Army uniform, I didn't play
girl games, don't look at me. My little boy is getting distracted by
the dildoes at the sex shop I try to hustle him past. Soon enough he'll
learn to leave his dress at home, will hear somewhere that a boy in a dress
cannot be beautiful. Once inside our

house he undresses by the mirror to be naked under the dress,
and lifts it up to display what most of us keep inside our
pants, and he asks me, a little afraid for the answer, *Am I beautiful, Dad —*

Feel a certain power over you dead I don't want—

Nashvillanelle

I've told you everything I have to say;
Now go. You're like that truck-stop country song,
How can I miss you, when you won't go away? —

The one that, wishing you'd laugh, I used to play
On air guitar the summer we came unstrung.
I've told you everything I have to say:

Lie down and rest. Deny it as you may,
You're dead, you know. I saw you die. So long.
How can I miss you when you won't go away?

I place such trust that, placed the proper way,
The right words make things right, but am I wrong?
I've told you everything I have to say,

Expecting what? A way with words to outweigh
Your way with silence, that's so final and so strong?
How can I miss you when you won't go away?

You linger as if death's cast you astray,
The same as life. Is there no place you belong?
I've told you everything I have to say.
How can I miss you, when you won't go away?

Outside there is a kind of rain that doesn't fall, a light
that, Godlike, is and isn't there, not brightening, not dying away —
It's your birthday, love, and we sleep late
together inside separate dreams of trouble, the sea half the day
skidding and pulling at the edge of our waking minds like love
that is given and taken back — dreams of the undeparted dead,

frightened skulls of ancestors on Day of the Dead
altars surrounded by saints and sugar candy and candlelight,
mangled replays of old fights with Dad about loving men, loving
you — he says, *I understand with you — what you call it — the way
you live — I know it's a hopeless case* — but today is the feast-day
of hopeless cases, lost causes, the never-to-be and the too-late-

for-help, the day of St. Jude, the patron of his belated
prayers of vengeance and regret. No matter: whatever kind of case Dad
was he isn't any more: we are faithful and alive today,
but he is dead, a cast of light in my eyes that blocks the light
of day, a presence of the past. I could let it die away
now on its own, that glare of *no* and *no*, that way of thinking love

itself is hopeless, not meant for me; when you say you love
me, I could let it be the truth. Outside our door, look, late-
morning fog has half-erased the world as if we've been borne away
to another in our sleep, trailing clouds of glory from the land of the dead
and waking in the cloud of our unknowing, ourselves each other's light.
Come walk with me and greet the day:

the air is sweet and promising, quiet and full, because it's the day
you were born. Are you afraid, even after love
has saved my life, that I won't love you back? So little light
before us, but of not knowing there is no end: too late
to know why on and on, back through the ages of the dead,
the fathers have unloved their sons, but let God keep them now, and far away

from us, St. Jude, I pray — *A Jew no less,* he says — *gone and thrown away*
your Catholic faith. Baruch atah Adonai: and let God separate the day
from the night. No point in fighting with the dead
but still I do; no point in owning a human heart, love,
but still I want one. There could be a kind of freedom in it, to let
the hopeless cases be, but we pray when hope is gone. Even the daylight

today is dark, even the ocean sends forth its dead,
wave after wave, to accumulate at our feet — it can't be stopped. Light
fails, death lives, and love, which is helpless, saves our lives anyway.

Faint music

You have been traveling farther
while I work and sleep, traveling faster,
driving your ship of death
down the interstate highway you built
when you were alive and now I can
barely see or hear you, you are becoming
gone, becoming alone,
thinking of nothing, staring,
steering through eternal days of hail
or storms of sun or do you think of me,
and is that how you appeared in my dream
all at once one more time in the night
then fled, making the stern face
that could become a grin if you let it
but you don't and keep going,
gripping the wheel with your left
and fingering the knobs and dials worn smooth as pearls
with your right, reaching for a voice,
some human Muzak drone you won't
have to listen to as you drive
but as you and the world you made
grow forgotten from each other the signals go weak,
leaving you unbound as you always wanted to be,
nothing but horizon down this open stretch
because now is the beginning of death,
and there is no one to touch,
and I am almost out of your reach.

(blue)

Through the days of driving home from burying you
whole hours I was dead, looking not seeing,

everything around so occupied with
continuing to live, prairie turning to desert plain,

to foothill and forest, and to this high valley,
a mountain turned inside out by heat

forced ages of ages ago from far below the rock,
white rock smoothed as if by hand and colored red-to-green

by the smallest forms of life at the edge of boiling water,
the hottest water blue — it too continued, coming forth

like the blue of your violent eyes in my mind,
because the motion of life-in-death has never stopped,

but life could not reach me — whole hours I was dead,
most of all to the ones who insisted on giving me love.

(faithful)

Waiting with the others for the expected eruption —
a teasing burst at four o'clock then nothing,

like anger that cools too soon —
thirty years ago you brought me here, a day we had to stay

and watch it go three times, each time an hour between
of almost laughable dread, standing out of your way

because it was not what you wanted —
too much steam in front of the water

or not enough, a certain unshapeliness
that offended you, or sun glare, something —

who'd have dared to ask *Can't you just look?*
And as I began to think the mesmerized crowd

wasn't facing the truth, that the little spurt we'd seen was all,
over before half begun, there came a huge and high

spouting for minutes impossible to believe
though I had seen it myself, three times before,

and behind this pillar of cloud a ridge of forest
half burned half green, lines of life climbing the air

the great fires hadn't touched or touched barely,
the lines of devastation and endlessness....

Though the crowd lost interest and dispersed
it continued on, the little banneret of steam

a reminder and an omen, unending,
though you were now nine days gone —

(ghost)

In the morning I felt lighter, freer,
we packed up peaceably, we drove away,

and heading north around Mt. Washburn
the swaths of grey and blackened trees up hillsides

and over meadows moved me,
I began to cry again, missing you,

I wanted you to see where greenness came back
the very next spring, the seeds and bulbs unscarred

an inch below ground, hardly any life
ever truly destroyed, pine cones opening in the flames —

it could have made me believe in the resurrection,
but we passed, between Norris and Canyon, through one

of the dead zones, the ghost-patches of sterilized ground.
Enough to say, as it is useless to call a force of nature

harmful or good, that you had passed over and gone
yet remained to me, necessary as you are.

a rift, a fault, a break in relation-
ship, an opening, an open space

Before words

A baby is singing in the morning
before anyone is up in the house

Before he has decided
which of all the languages he will speak
he is trying the sounds of his voice
in the first light

He hears a man
come up the street collecting bottles
just ahead of the garbage truck
straining uphill
to come throw them away

He hears the shriek of glass
It is like the vessels of Creation
breaking in God's hands

He hears the wind around the house
and in the wind
every word he will ever say
and what will stay unsaid

and stops to listen to silence
and sings to it
the way the body addresses the soul
lending it shape
lending it comfort and sorrow

The body wants to be useful
and the soul is open so wide

This is the way we awaken
He remembers he is alone
and cries for us.

Second son | *St. Louis, 1947*

They are posing in front of the '46 Kaiser, the sharpest car
his Dad's ever had, *dolled up like gangsters going*
God knows where, her mother, behind the camera, snaps — *someplace*
decent girls go I certainly hope, and turns her
back, and walks into the house. *Act like she ain't half afraid*
of me, he huffs, straightening his hat — *Tell me enough*

times already that sly way of hers I'm not good enough.
When he presses my mother to his side at the car
door her smile gets a kind of scold in it, *and is she afraid*
of me a little too, or scared of life, and how am I going
to tell her marry me scared half foolish of her
myself? But she settles into place

beside him as a breeze stirs up, and places
a hand at her hair, a little shy, a little daring, just enough
of a sign of a chance with her
he can beg one kiss, leaning her tighter against the car
door and feeling stronger, feeling she is going
to tell him yes, seeing as how she's not afraid

of her mother at the window watching, not even afraid
of the roughness of his hands. *Coarse little hick from no place*
drives a truck for a living — he knows her folks aren't going
to stand for him, he knows through and through he isn't good enough.
Always been the second son. He's spent all morning polishing his father's car
and dressed himself up in a shirt and tie for her

and these creased wool pants; she is wearing her
best black dress held open low with a silver clasp. *I'm afraid*
you're right, Ma, we's gangsters now, and this here car's
our getaway, he winks — *get ourselves any place*
we can away from you, no place far enough.
It's a cool summer afternoon and tonight is going

to be the night, but I'm afraid I can't tell you where they're going
to next — I have only this photograph of Grandma's I stole out her
scrapbook years ago because my Dad looked beautiful enough
in it to love, contented in a way I don't recall. I'm afraid
I'm making up a story. I'm afraid what happens next. Someplace
beautiful, a high bluff maybe where they can watch the river pass, he pulls the car

over to ask my mother his question and place a pledge of love in her
hand. The car idles at the cliff — but what would there be for her to feel afraid
of? He is going to love her forever. It's his second son he will not love enough.

An island of white oak and red oak, cottonwood and red bud, a barge
　　　at Utica passing through the locks,

the petroleum and LP trucks warming up in the lot of the farm service
　　　bureau, the drivers blowing into their hands and pulling on gloves
　　　for the day's work,

a tarpaper house on stilts over the floodplain, a chimney covered with
　　　vines, a line of cypresses leaning to the river, a girl riding her bike
　　　with training wheels down the field of grass,

a tilting white cottage under the sandstone bluffs, a haymow, a hog pen, a
　　　swingset, a satellite dish,

prefab aluminum granaries, plastic lawn deer, cornflowers, bees and
　　　horseflies in the roadside grass and bickering starlings, three
　　　pickups crossing the ferry at Kampsville, the rural electrification
　　　plant,

water sprayed into a field from a soaker hose unwound from a heavy
　　　spool,

herbicide sprayed from a tank under the air-conditioned tractor and
　　　accumulating in the black soil, turning up years later in the
　　　drinking water at the bottom of the page in a newspaper report,

a boy and his father on their knees working in dirt, turning plowed-under
　　　scrub to grass and shrubbery with little patterns of gravel and
　　　stepping-stones, clearing away the pungent weeds that green the
　　　skin,

a freshly dug well, the raised welt from the backhoe running in a line
　　　all the way to the house and a man looking at his work, mud up both
　　　arms to the shoulder,

a red-tailed hawk, a turkey vulture, the gray feathers fluttering and parting
        on an owl's throat, the bird cooling itself in the midday heat,

a boarded-up gas station and machine shop, a rusted two-wheel oil tank
        leaning on its handle under the maple tree, two mobile homes
        and a tractor in front of a sagging, windowless farmhouse at
        Pearl,

black bears and wolves gone from this country like the Kickapoo, the
        Illinois, the Fox,

a hulking farm dog barking at the road long after the car has passed,

a quarry of lime and red rock, a road crew leaning at a steamroller to
        smoke,

the heat pausing, the air moist and sweet, the heavens pulling in a long
        breath and cutting loose a clattering downpour over and done in
        ten minutes then hauling back the sun, so that the fields steam
        again and the soaked trees sweat,

the county courthouse with a clock for each direction on the skullcapped
        square tower, the brick homes and clapboards through town
        along Route 4 with stone-pillared wraparound porches, the finest
        mansion in town a funeral home,

cousins playing catch at the family reunion while they wait for the birthday
        cake, the youngest baby standing himself up on unsteady feet on
        the blanket spread out in the shade, patting the trunk of the
        sycamore,

a man in Schuyler County estranged from his wife who takes his boys
        aged two and four out in the car and shoots them in the head by
        the side of the road near Rushville, then shoots himself, the
        younger boy safely strapped into his car seat in the back,

an auto graveyard, a Meadow Gold Dairy truck upended without wheels, a
gravel pit, two wagon wheels at a driveway dotted with reflector
caps,

a birdhouse in the shape of a riverboat, paper trash smoking in a burn
barrel, a brown-spotted coyote crossing the road, a one-lane
bridge,

generations of washing machines and oil cans, mower blades and truck
parts, piled in a neat square patch in back of the house and
overgrown with tall grass,

Hardee's and Taco Bell and Target and Wal-Mart, all new, floating in
acres of parking under the tall lights, the edge of the city
spreading into the flat darkness,

a grassland scraped flat by a thousand years of ice, teeming, passive,
forgiving, unprepared, the richest soil on earth,

a drawbridge missing green paint in the section that had to be repaired,
and a farmer sitting in his truck waiting to cross, patiently reading
the death notices in the county paper, one hand on the wheel,

a yellow band of wheat, and bands of darker and lighter green in the bean
and corn fields down the slope to the river, and the sun falling
open over the riverbank woods.

Brightness

Driving home from the hospice, from his death,
four a.m. now, his last possessions in a paper bag
beside me on the seat, the heavy glasses,
the teeth in a margarine tub,
his cheap watch on my arm as though I'd stolen
time back, the smell of his skin
on my hands; over the city
where I was born there's a sliver
of glass, the new moon
with the old moon in its arms;
so dark, and no one on the streets
as if this were my dream city
that I won't have to share with anyone,
enclosed apart in its own time
but a little changed, a little decayed
from the way I remember it, separate
from me after all, going its own way; it is not
my memory; time has not stopped; my father is dead.
O ferocious soul with your famous mistrust of love,
I think your darkness
must be my inheritance;
I reach the edge of the city, drive west on Highway 36
and there is no one under the shelter of darkness
but me and two or three truckers on the road,
early risers like you, starting the working day
before anyone has stirred; so the far past
returns and you come into my room softly
to tap me out of sleep
in the dark, we go for a ride in the truck
somewhere, you and me, shivering awake, our breath visible,
alone in our bodies,
alone in the world.

The *California Poetry Series* celebrates the great diversity of aesthetics, culture, geography, and ethnicity of the state by publishing work by poets with strong ties to California. Books within this series are published quarterly and feature the work of a single poet, or in some cases two or more poets with a clear affinity. Malcolm Margolin of Heyday Books is publisher; Joyce Jenkins of Poetry Flash is editor.

An advisory board of prominent poets and other cultural leaders has been assembled to help support the series. These include Alfred Arteaga, Chana Bloch, Christopher Buckley, Marilyn Chin, Karen Clark, Wanda Coleman, Gillian Conoley, Peter Coyote, Jim Dodge, Lawrence Ferlinghetti, Jack Foley, Jewelle Gomez, Robert Hass, Jane Hirshfield, Fanny Howe, Lawson Inada, Jaime Jacinto, Diem Jones, Stephen Kessler, William Kistler, Carolyn Kizer, Steve Kowit, Dorianne Laux, Philip Levine, Genny Lim, Suzanne Lummis, Lewis MacAdams, David Mas Masumoto, David Meltzer, Deena Metzger, Carol Muske, Jim Paul, Kay Ryan, Richard Silberg, Gary Snyder, Dr. Kevin Starr, David St. John, Sedge Thomson, Alan Williamson, and Gary Young.

Books in the *California Poetry Series* are available at bookstores nationwide or by subscription. For more information contact:
California Poetry Series
c/o The Roundhouse Press
P.O. Box 9145
Berkeley, California 94709
phone: 510.549.3564   fax: 510.549.1889
e-mail: roundhouse@heydaybooks.com

CALIFORNIA POETRY SERIES

1